from Busy to Productive

JAIME SAURET

Copyright © 2024 Jaime Sauret.

All rights reserved.

ISBN: 9798324021672

No part of this book may be reproduced, distributed, or transmitted in any form or by any means, including photocopying, recording, or other electronic or mechanical method, without the prior written permission of the publisher or author, except in case of brief quotations embodied in reviews and certain non-commercial uses permitted by copyright law.

Book cover by Yasir Nadeem.

DEDICATION

I want to dedicate this book to:

MY WIFE

Who has been my support day and night and has been there from beginning to end. She was (and still is) encouraging me on the grey days and cheering me up on the sunny ones. This book will not be in your hands without her.

MY MOM

My forever fan #1. She has always supported my dreams and ambitions and is the best example I have on how to overcome any challenge. If I have to choose who is my role model on how to adapt to any change and make the best out of any circumstance, no one can take her place.

MY DAD

Not here anymore but I know he would be so proud and happy to see this work. He taught me that the question is not 'how easy can it be' but 'how hard I should push' to make it happen.

MY DOGS

Last but not least: Loly, Tonnie and Milky. They are and will always be my daily reminder to love, live and enjoy life today.

FOREWORD

By Dr. Dag Piper

In a world that often confuses motion with progress, Jaime's insightful book emerges as a clear call to recalibrate our understanding of true productivity. *From Busy to Productive* isn't merely a book; it's a gateway to a transformative journey that redefines the essence of how we work and live.

With wisdom as profound as it is practical, Jaime peels back the layers of what it truly means to be busy. Whether you find yourself perpetually racing against the clock, or simply trying to make your hours count for more, this book promises to be a faithful companion. Through personal anecdotes, sharp observations, and actionable advice, Jaime equips us not just to do more, but to be more.

This book isn't just about managing time; it's about understanding what truly deserves your energy.

Welcome to your new beginning.

Dr. Dag Piper
Director Future and Growth Initiatives @ ISI
Inspirational and endless curios leader in FMCG industry

CONTENT

INTRODUCTION..1

PART 1. TIME

01. CONTROL YOUR TIME = CONTROL YOUR DAY.........12
02. GATHER 18
03. ORGANIZE 24
04. ACTION...32

PART 2. ENERGY

05. NO ENERGY = NO DO 40
06. THE POWER OF BREAKS 46
07. HOW ABOUT SAYING NO? 52
08. BE MOODY 58

PART 3. FOCUS

09. NO FOCUS = WASTED TIME & ENERGY 66
10. DISTRACTIONS 72
11. PRIORITIES 76
12. FIND YOUR FLOW 82

PART 4. GROWTH

13. KNOWLEDGE IS FREEDOM 90
14. LEARNING 96
15. YOU VS. YOU 102
16. TALENT OR EFFORT? 108

PART 5. NOW WHAT?

17. THE B2P SYSTEM 116
18. BONUS CHAPTER 124

FURTHER READING 139
ACKNOWLEDGEMENTS 141

A new way...

...for old productivity

INTRODUCTION

> *"Productivity is being able to do things that you were never able to do before"*
>
> *- Franz Kafka*

What if I told you can be in control of your days?

Easy, right? but why has it always been one of the biggest challenges we all face?

World is busier than ever, and it's pretty likely that is not going to slow down. We are connected in a way that our grandparents couldn't even dream about. We can get answers in seconds, we are reachable with just one click, technology has made our jobs way easier and able to deal with more stuff at the same time. We are living in the Jetsons[1] world.

---

[1] American animated sitcom produced by Hanna-Barbera Productions in the 1960s

However, there was a time with no online chats or email on your phone.

I'm not sure if people were more productive back then. I'm not even sure if people were talking about productivity the same way we are talking about it today, or at all. What I can tell you is this: Productivity is one of the best skills a person can have and ironically one of the most misunderstood of the last years. Everybody wants to be productive, a lot of people think they are, but only a few are actually there. Why? Because people believe being productive means to be busy… and I was one of them.

Productivity has changed my life forever. It gives me freedom to enjoy my time and feeling full of energy to work on the things that are important for me.

But it was not always like that.

I've been working on understanding consumers for almost 2 decades, which means I've been involved on tons of projects during that time. And for at least half of the time, when someone asked me the typical question *'hey, how are you?'* my answer was always *'busy, you know how it is'*. I was so proud about it! Was like a badge, a confirmation that I was killing it and on top of everything.

In reality I was always behind, jumping from one task to another and running to meetings in between: meetings to align, pre-align, post-align, re-align, checking emails during the day while doing other things, reacting to requests from other people and working on as many things as I can possibly do. And that was just work.

I always had personal goals and dreams, always wanted to do more, same as you and probably half of the people on this planet. I've always started my years with the typical resolution that I'll exercise more, read more, cook more. I've always wanted to write a book and promised to myself that I'd start. But I never started any of them. At the end of every single day, I felt exhausted, with my tank empty.

I was not moving forward neither at work nor in my personal life. I was in reacting mode going with the flow.

Sounds familiar?

At some point I said enough. I made the decision to change my reality and start being in control of my work and my days. That was the moment when I started learning everything I could about productivity. I was a sponge!

And you know what? Best thing I've ever done. I'm now in control not only of my days but my life! I even changed the '*I'm busy*' for *'I'm being productive'*

WHAT DOES IT MEAN TO BE PRODUCTIVE?

Let me start with the most important fact about productivity:

<u>YOU</u>
<u>OWN</u>
<u>YOUR TIME!!</u>

Does this mean that you need to wake up at 4am and work like a robot the whole day?

Absolutely… not!

We've all read how successful people manage their days taking account of every minute of their agenda or how this or that CEO wakes up at 4:20am and by 7am, when people are waking up, they have half of her priorities done. All those stories are great to inspire people to change, but how realistic are they? How do normal people like us can do something like that and win our days?

We live in a crazy busy world with an extreme demand for our attention and lots of things pulling from every direction. People still believe that the more things you do at the same time the better, or working moving from one task to another for 8 hours non-stop filling every minute of your time with something makes you a productive person.

CRAZY FACT

Did you know research suggests that you are productive only around 2 hours and 53 min in an eight-hour day? [2]

And how about the people that take pride in always working more? If you work more it does not mean you get more done or you care more. It just means… well… that you just work more.

Let's get back to what it means to be productive.

---

[2] Inc magazine: In an 8-Hour Day, the Average Worker Is Productive for This Many Hours | Inc.com

I'M AT WAR WITH PRODUCTIVITY APPS

The first thing you need to know about productivity: forget about apps, software, websites and tools. To be productive you only need 2 things: a notebook and a calendar (a pen might be handy as well).

I'm not a big fan of apps and software for productivity. Don't get me wrong, they are extremely helpful, and now with AI you can do wonders automating recurrent tasks, linking calendars and managing projects with your team. I actually recommend you to take advantage of AI and new tools to enjoy their benefits.

The challenge is that our culture it's linked to tools instead of principles and behavior. This makes people go in a never-ending quest on getting the 'best' app or the latest software that will magically solve their life (spoiler alert, they won't).

The second thing you need to know: what productivity is not. Productivity is not about how busy you are, how many tasks can you complete or how many meetings you can attend in a day. It's not even how good you are managing your time.

How many times have you felt tired, mentally drained and like someone else is in control of your days? It's so common to feel like this, almost on a daily basis.

There are new definitions that include managing your energy as well, which it's a great improvement, but it goes even deeper.

After tons of books and thousands of articles I could find about productivity, studying the gurus of time management and people that are extremely productive and trying to figure out what is it that they all have in common to 'kill it' every day, you know what I've learned? That productivity it's like a house with 4 pillars: Time, Energy, Focus, Growth.

So yes, productivity it's about managing your time efficiently and managing your energy to be at your best physically and mentally during the day. But it's also about managing your focus to invest that energy in the best way possible and managing your knowledge so you know how to do what you have to do. If productivity was a recipe, it would have four ingredients: Time as the base ingredient, and Energy, Focus and Growth to add flavor.

Now, how would you feel if you were in control of your days and all the things you have to do, with energy left in the tank at the end of your day to do things you enjoy or work on something that you are passionate about? Imagine how your life would be. Do you believe it's possible?

If you do, you are right!

If you don't, I want to challenge you and prove you wrong. I will help you to be in the driver seat of every single day of your life. **I want to help you to MOVE FROM BUSY TO PRODUCTIVE**.

In the last part of the book, I share the system I created that has helped me, my family, friends, colleagues and people I've coached to make that jump from busy to productive, or as I call it: **THE B2P SYSTEM**.

Yes, you could jump to the last part and implement the system, no guilt in that. In fact, I invite you to do that so you can start your productivity journey today.

But if you take the following pages as a personal experiment rather than just words in a book, you'll end up having a life-changing experience and will start to be in control of your days, and your life.

My intention is not to give you the ultimate answer or a magical pill that will change your life overnight, because I don't believe it exists. Or to pretend that I know all there is to know about productivity, because I don't.

I wrote this book to help you navigate the busyness of this world. There are tons of books for each ingredient of the productivity recipe, but I haven't found one that combines all. And that's what I want to give you: one place where you have all the basic ingredients for you to cook your own productivity recipe.

I believe we all have the right to own our time and decide how we want to invest it for the life we want. As Darren Hardy said *'You don't need to learn anything more. You don't need new information; you need a new plan of action'*[3].

In your hands right now, you have years of my life, my notes, the battles I fought and what I have suffered and enjoyed to find a solution to the busyness pandemic of today. So use it, share it and enjoy it!

Live by design, not by default.

WELCOME TO THE B2P LIFE!

---

[3] Darren Hardy, *The Compound Effect* Book

PART 1

Time

01

CONTROL YOUR TIME

=

CONTROL YOUR DAY

CHAPTER 1

"Time is what we want most, but what we use is worst"

- William Penn

It was a Thursday afternoon, moving from one meeting to another like any other day at work, when finally, it was time for my performance review. I was so excited this time. We went into a meeting room, closed the door and my boss started: *Jaime, you had a good quarter. You always have great ideas and your results are where they should be, but there's a timing problem. You are always behind, tend to take longer to deliver what's needed and miss deadlines quite often'.*

I was devastated! I was working so hard for the last months and this was totally unexpected.

This feedback opened my eyes: I understood I was not at my best, I needed to change. But this EUREKA moment was not immediate, far from it! I was in denial for months. I was complaining about how unfair my boss was: *'wait a minute, how is this possible? How is it that I'm always doing lots of things and attending meetings but still behind? No way, they don't know what they are talking about'.*

It took me time (love the irony of this!) and hitting some walls in the process to fully bring to light that the problem was not my results but with my time (later I realized it was more than that, but more to come in part 2). It was when I started to be honest with myself that I could look at the feedback with a more objective lens. And you know what I discovered? It was true!

I learned 2 extremely important lessons: 1) I was working on too many things at the same time; and 2) I was giving my time away being busy with other's priorities instead of investing it on my own projects and responsibilities. The solution was pretty obvious.

I started to work on my priorities first, one at a time. At the beginning I moved the needle, but after a couple of months I felt stuck again. I felt the needle was not moving anymore and that my time was still going somewhere else, that it was not *my time* anymore.

I spent months thinking about this and how I could really change it. And after almost a year I decided that I needed to change the strategy again. Putting my priorities first was not the only key. I read tons of books, online articles, corporate magazines, blogs, online training, YouTube videos... you name it. Every piece of information I could put my hands on I ate it. And that's when I discovered the 2 biggest truths about productivity: **YOU OWN YOUR TIME** and that **PRODUCTIVITY IS NOT ONLY ABOUT TIME**. Ironic, isn't it?

You've probably already felt like you are not in control of your days. If you got this book it is because you are looking to change that too and very likely you have the same question I had: how the hell do I do it?

WORK ON YOUR AGENDA, NOT OTHERS'

This one sounds obvious, but is one of the hardest. And it's hard because we love to feel important.

You know what you have to do but that email you just saw from the director is urgent, and that weekly meeting is so important. Maybe it is. But what usually happens? You end up postponing your project reacting to the "urgencies" of the day.

We let other people decide what goes into our agendas. We go to back-to-back-to-back-to-back meetings and when -or if- we have some extra minutes we check our emails or reply to chat messages. We are constantly in reaction mode. No wonder why at the end of your days you feel that you did a lot but end up nowhere.

It's ok and part of the game to help others, but people will always have questions about their priorities, not yours. They set time for meetings when it's convenient for them, not you. You probably won't like this, but being in meetings doesn't make you more important.

Putting your priorities first doesn't mean now you are not going to help anyone anymore and work in an island. Teamwork is essential. Yes, I still support my team and help when it is needed and I attend the (actual) important meetings, but I always put my projects first. It's like the oxygen mask approach in airplanes: help yourself first so you can help others.

You might be thinking *'what about urgencies?'* Yes, they do exist and are always going to be there, but that does not mean you have to react to all of them all the time in the same way. Let's read that one again: **that does not mean**

you have to react to all of them all the time in the same way.

You can invest time to solve real urgencies, but believe me that 92,7% of the urgencies you see each day are not really that urgent. Take a minute before reacting to everything that comes your way and ask yourself: is this really urgent? Sounds silly, but works wonders.

Time is the most valuable asset we have but is the one we are the worst taking care of. You probably have heard a million times *'Time is money'*. I kind of like the analogy, but I don't think it's accurate. If you lose money, you can get it back. But if you lose time, it's gone forever. This is why time is the first ingredient.

But what's the secret to owning your time? To manage it efficiently. You do it not by saving time, but by MAKING time for what you want and need to do.

How to make time? With a simple 3-step process:

GO-ACT → **G**ather, **O**rganize, **ACT**ion.

And like walking, let's start with the first step.

02

GATHER

CHAPTER 2

> *"Give me six hours to chop down a tree and I will spend the first four sharpening the axe"*
>
> *- (attributed to) Abraham Lincoln*

This is the preparation phase, or THE WHAT, and one of the most important steps (if not the most) in the productivity journey. You could do everything else to perfection, but if you fail to prepare your productivity will always be incomplete.

I've always thought that planning was the key for productivity. At the beginning, when I decided to embark on my productivity journey, my days started planning tasks as they came. I would open my computer, check my email and plan my day. It worked for a while, but after a few months I realized I was reacting to whatever was on my inbox. So, I changed my strategy.

I started my days making a list of tasks and picking from that list to book them in my calendar. Just that small change was a huge improvement to move away from reacting to other people's priorities. But after another couple of months, I felt that something was still missing. Yes, I was way more productive than before, but I was feeling I was still reacting to things happening around me. I felt I was not where I wanted to be, where I knew I could be.

It was when I started preparing before planning that I saw the real change. I had full clarity on what I needed to plan. It may sound obvious, but in reality is not because we are not familiar with what it means to prepare your day.

Let's do a quick exercise: if I ask you to prepare your week now, what would you do? Take your time.

Most likely you thought about the things you have to do and (maybe) decide when you'll do each. But that's not really preparation.

Do you remember all the things you have to do? Have full clarity on your priorities? Which actions will move you closer to your objectives?

WHAT'S PREPARATION THEN?

It goes beyond finding time to complete tasks. It's understanding what you have to do and which tasks are the most critical for your goals.

How does it work?

1. List all the projects and goals you have: work, personal, family.

2. Pick your 3 most important goals or projects.

3. Take one of those goals and list all the actions that will help you to make it happen.

4. Repeat step 3 for the other 2 goals.

One of the keys to preparation is to have a list.

Our brain is a mysterious machine. It's great at processing information but is not that reliable at remembering everything we have to do. Don't believe me? When do you remember to buy the batteries of the TV remote, when you are doing the groceries or when you want to turn on the TV?

However, having a list just for the sake of listing all your tasks helps but is not enough. The typical to-do list has changed, evolved to do more than just help. It frees your mind to do what it's made for, to think, create and brainstorm, instead of just storing information. Your mind can't do its job if it's overwhelmed by constantly thinking and trying to remember all the things you have to do.

A LIST IS YOUR HERO!

But why having 1 hero if you can have 2?

That's why I recommend having 2 lists: a **MASTER LIST** to help you with the big picture, and an **ACTION LIST** for your tasks to help you with the preparation.

How are they connected with the gather phase? During the steps above, you make your **MASTER LIST** in step 1, and your **ACTION LIST** helps you with steps 3 & 4.

Now you have THE WHAT.

Next step: THE WHEN.

03

ORGANIZE

CHAPTER 3

"An hour of planning can save you 10 hours of doing"

- Dale Carnegie

Time for THE WHEN.

And talking about when...

One Saturday morning, while waiting for my coffee to be ready, I found a blog post about how successful people plan their days for maximum productivity. Lots of information on how they do it: waking up at 3:45am and by 7:09am they have already half their life figured it out.

My personal problem with that is that I'm not a morning person, it is not in my DNA. I've heard that before, tried it but has been always impossible for me. How can I become a productive person if I can't wake up at 3:45am? But one piece of advice caught my attention, one that I've never seen until that morning: **they plan their week in advance.**

At the beginning I didn't give too much credit to be honest. Few weeks passed by and then I remembered it again, and decided to give it a try. I booked some time next Sunday afternoon to plan my week. I took my ACTION LIST, picked the 5 most immediate actions for that week… and it was like magic!

That was the best week I had in years. I did more during that week than in the previous 12 months. Best of all, I started to feel like I was in control of my days. Finally!

Biggest learning about planning: your day starts… the day before.

But before moving to how to do the planning, I want to share one important fact. If there's only 1 thing you will take with you from this book and forget about all the rest, let it be this: **<u>YOUR CALENDAR IS YOUR BEST FRIEND</u>**. Your calendar it's your personal assistant, your defense against bad memory and your stress antidote.

HOW TO DO PLANNING?

The key for a great planning is not a complicated process or a super advanced software. It's just 3 easy steps:

1. Review your ACTION LIST.

2. Pick the most immediate actions you want to complete.

3. Book them in your calendar.

An open calendar might feel good as it makes you feel that you have all the free time you need, but an open calendar is a magnet for meetings and other people's priorities.

As your day starts the day before, you do the planning the night before. Just 5 minutes gives you the freedom to start your day on your own terms.

Want to take planning to the next level? I personally recommend to invest 10-15 min Friday before you close for the day and plan the full week ahead. All you need to do is repeat the 3-steps for each day of the week.

You know that feeling right before going on holiday? Why not having the same feeling every Friday before diving into the weekend?

You're probably thinking *'how about all the urgent things that I can't predict?'* True, urgencies will always be there, but it's way easier to adapt when needed and rearrange things than to solve all of them as they appear.

Want to take planning even further? Here some additional tips that will help you do the planning phase like a pro:

- **Too big, break it in pieces.** If an action or a project is too big, break it into smaller actions. Think of it as steps to get to what you want to complete. You need to prepare the end of year presentation? Book 1 section per day. Big projects are way scarier than simple actions.

- **(re)Think time**. Instead of trying to fit your actions in blocks of time, use the blocks of time as guides to measure the size of the actions. It's easier to adapt the action to a time assigned because we suck at predicting how long it takes to complete a task. Not sure how long to book? Don't sweat it, book 1 hour and adapt when needed. You will get better the more you do it.

- **Highlight of the day**. I learned this one from the book *Make Time* by Jake Knapp and IT CHANGED MY LIFE! When booking your tasks in your calendar think about this: *'what is that action that's critical or that will make me feel it was a productive day when I close?'* That's your highlight of the day. You can have other actions during the day, but that is your most important one.

- **Batch your action**. Stack actions from the same project as much as possible together. It's better to work on different actions for the same project for 4 days than jumping from one project to another. You'll complete your projects faster and manage better your energy (more about managing your energy in Part 2).

- **Have 1 no-meeting day**. Meetings are everywhere and you cannot control all of them, but you can decide which ones to attend. A no-meeting day gives you back a full day to recover. You might need to break this rule once in a while, but keep those days as an exception. If CEOs can do this, you can.

PRO TIP

SAVE A SPACE IN YOUR CALENDAR FOR URGENCIES

Book three 30-min slots at different days of your week and call it <u>urgencies</u>. If something pops up you take care of the urgency and move what you have planned to that 30-minute slot. If nothing happens, you have 30 extra minutes to dedicate to your priorities.

PICK YOUR PEAK TIME

I've heard a lot of people recommending starting the day with your most important task. They call it winning the day or 'eat the frog'. To be honest it's a good advice as it's based on the principle of working on your most important task when you have the most energy.

If you are the type of person that can wake up, wash your face and be up-and-running full speed first thing in the morning, this is going to be great for you.

The challenge I have with that advice is that is not for everybody. Not all of us are a morning person (as you already know, I am not) or feel full of energy right from sunrise. Are we losers if we don't eat our frogs first thing in the morning? Of course not.

What's the solution? **Pick your peak time**. That time when you feel the most energized.

For me, I need some time to get my system up and running in the morning (and some coffee). I start my days with some easy low energy tasks like emails and quick administrative tasks. It's around 10am when I plan my highlight of the day because that's when I am at my peak.

My advice is to do your highlight of the day when you are at your highest energy of the day. If it's in the afternoon, then that's your peak time.

A final thought: The point of planning is not to fill every minute of your day with things to do. The aim is to use time as a guide to move closer to your goals. Don't race against time, learn how to walk with it.

Now, time to take action.

04

ACTION

CHAPTER 4

"The way to get started is to quit talking and begin doing"

- Walt Disney

Ready... set... ACTION!

Preparing and planning are critical. There's always one more thing to plan, one more idea to consider. But without action your plan will stay on paper.

This is actually my biggest struggle. I love planning, thinking on the steps I need to take and finding the time to book each. But for some reason, when it's time for action-mode, my mind always has an excuse ready to use.

I am a big-time procrastinator. I have to fight it almost every day. Every time I have to do something, I start: *'well, I'm tired'* or *'let me plan it better so it's perfect'*. And the only thing I end up doing is... not doing what I have to. I brainstormed with myself and planned how it would be to write this book for almost a year, but I did not write a single word during that time!

Have you heard about paralysis by analysis? Well, I suffer paralysis by planning.

Fortunately, I found a concept that change my life and has help me to by-pass my excuses and move into action: *The 5 Second Rule*[4].

How does it work? Count from 5 to 1 out loud and go when reach 1. Time for your workout but you want to see one more episode of The Last of Us? 5-4-3-2-1 and take your a$$ out of the couch.

I know, sometimes you just don't feel like it, but I have bad news for you: you'll never feel like it. Our brain loves to relax and save energy but that's why this technique is so effective, because it puts you back in control over your mind.

I literally did it to draft this chapter… and to edit it… and to format it.

---

[4] Mel Robins, *The 5 Second Rule* Book.

NOW YOU HAVE THE SECRET TO TAKE ACTION

Well, no that fast my friend. You still have to move!

The bad news: you need to put effort.

THE GOOD NEWS: it's not impossible. It might feel a bit hard at the beginning, but once you get used to it I promise you it's a game changer.

And to help you to make taking action even easier here are 3 easy tricks:

- **Respect your time.** Commit with yourself: when the calendar reminder appears, do what you said you'll do. If you put it there, respect the time you invest planning it.

- **Progress over movement.** Don't confuse progress with movement. Planning helps to see how to get where you want to go and might make you feel like you are moving (well, you are doing something, right?), but action is the only one that will actually get you there.

- **Commit to the minimum**. It sounds weird, but bear with me for a second. I don't remember where I read it but it's one of those things that stayed with you forever: what is the minimum that you are willing to do that will help you to move the needle? Commit to that. 9 times out of 10 you'll do more because you'll feel you want to do more. Our mind is a beautiful and weird thing.

PRO TIP

THE 2 MIN RULE

Does it take less than 2 min to do it? Do it now! Don't invest too much time in actions that don't need it.

What about individual actions that are not necessarily part of my projects? Same principle: less than 2 min? Go! More time? Book it.

Remember the GO-ACT process from chapter 1? Use it every day and you'll see how your productivity goes from 0X to 100X in just a week. Don't believe me? Give it a try and see it by yourself.

*

Congratulations on covering the first ingredient of your productivity recipe. Some cooking still to do.

Do you remember what's the second ingredient?

PART 2

Energy

05

NO ENERGY = NO DO

CHAPTER 5

"Energy, not time, is the fundamental currency of high performance"

- Jim Loehr

Productivity is not only about managing your time. If Time is the first ingredient, right there in second place comes Energy. You could have all the time in the world, but without energy there's no do.

Just like you (and millions of other people) I had tons of things I wanted to do: I have several projects at work but also wanted to write a book, exercise more, read more, learn how to cook. The problem was that I was exhausted after work. I thought what I needed was just some rest so I took a week off to recharge. I was so excited about all the things I planned to do after that break.

Sunday evening I sat down, wrote down all the things I had to do and booked them on my calendar. Monday started and everything was exactly as I planned it. But I was exhausted again by Wednesday! Some days I was done after lunch and others even from the moment I woke up. It was so frustrating. I knew what I had to do and the planning was perfect but for some reason I kept postponing them.

It was a vicious cycle: gather-organize-tired-postpone-break-gather-organize-tired-postpone-break.

After months of frustration I took the time to reflect and asked myself *'why am I feeling this way?'* And then, EUREKA! My tank was empty. I was a master managing my time but I was mentally exhausted.

That's when I started to pay attention to my energy and… BAM! After just 2 weeks I was working out regularly, cooked (almost) every day and STARTED TO WRITE MY FIRST BOOK (yes, this beauty you have now in your hands).

WE NEED TO STOP

We can't work non-stop for 8 hours and then go home and expect to do other things. When was the last time you took a break at work to recharge? No, talking with Rebecca about work over a coffee is not a proper break.

It's so hard to just stop working. How can you stop working with so many things you have to do?

But you can!

You don't need to take a month in the Bahamas once a year to recharge (even though it helps). Small steps consistently take you way further than one big leap once in a while.

I have 3 principles that will make you a master of managing your energy. I call them the BBM recharge combo: Breaks, Boundaries, Mood. And that's what the next 3 chapters are all about.

But you know what? Let's take a break and get a coffee -or tea- before we continue. Your body and mind will thank you for it. No phone, no emails, no TV: take your favorite cup, sit on your favorite spot and see you in 10 min!

Welcome back!

How do you feel?

I bet you feel more energized than 10 min ago.

Before jumping into the first BBM principle, let me share the 2 typical scenarios you'll face when feeling tired:

1. **Physically OK but not mentally = ready to go but no inspiration**. You might not feel tired but you cannot think properly. What to do? take regular breaks (more in next chapter).

2. **Mentally OK but not physically = high inspiration but wanted to sleep**. What to do? You guessed it: get enough sleep, eat well and exercise regularly.

To reach what you want you need to be at your best both physically and mentally. The challenge is that your brain is still primitive and it believes that its job is to keep you safe. It's programmed to spend the least amount of energy possible so you can run for your life if needed. If it has to choose between working out or staying on the couch watching another episode of The Last of Us, you already know which wins.

That's why you can let your brain be the one deciding. You have to be the one in control to work on what's important for you without your brain making you feel like you are wasting energy.

But the question is… where to start?

06

THE POWER OF BREAKS

CHAPTER 6

―――――――――

"There is virtue in work and there is virtue in rest. Use both and overlook neither"

- Alan Cohen

How many days have you worked non-stop in the last month? Be honest.

And how many days have you taken a break during the day? And I mean a real break, not just getting water from the water cooler in the office.

If I have to guess I'll bet you have done it maybe a couple of times a week, but far from regularly. That's what we all do. We all face our days head on, moving from one task to another and meetings in-between until it's time to close. I know because I was like that too.

I was managing my time to perfection; everything was planned and in place. I even had urgencies under control. But at the end of the day, I was exhausted. I thought that was a good sign, a sign that I was working hard.

So, I tried to compensate by sleeping more on the weekend, but it didn't help at all. I wanted to do so much but my tank was so empty. I was so frustrated!

I was in that doing-mode non-stop for years, busy with lots of things. But you know what I was not? Productive!

I needed to change that, so I started to look for information on how to do it, and the more I read the more I found the same answer: **take breaks during the day**.

I decided to give it a chance and it was the best decision ever! I started taking one break during the afternoon and in just a couple of weeks I felt so much better. I had a ton of energy after work to work on my personal projects. I did more in one month than what I was able to do in the previous year… while taking time to rest!

YOU ARE NOT A ROBOT

We all believe we are machines, but it's not only our fault. Thanks to technology we are hyper connected and everything moves extremely fast. What took weeks 40 years ago now takes only seconds. Imagine your work with no internet, no email and no cellphone.

But working like a machine is just setting yourself to fail. It's against our nature. When your brain starts to feel the tank empty it loses focus and gives in to any distraction. It doesn't want to burn the few energy it has left. No car moves with an empty tank.

Would you let your phone go to 0% battery? Of course not. We charge our phone when we see the battery in yellow. Why not doing the same with yourself?

You need to recharge -same as your phone- to regain some of the energy you used. You need to take a pause from the daily madness, a moment to breathe, rest and then continue.

How do you do that? Making breaks part of your daily routine. And you do that with 3 simple hacks:

- **Small breaks to refresh.** 5 min do magic. Stretch, stand up, go for water, wash your face. Make it a habit to do a quick stop in between tasks to refresh your eyes from your screen. Leave back-to-back to sports.

- **Big breaks to recharge.** 5 min refresh your eyes, but you also need to recharge. Stop 'working' for 15-min mid-morning and 15-min mid-afternoon. No email, no review of that mid-year report. Catch up with colleagues over a coffee, call a friend, or just sit somewhere and relax.

- **Don't fill your plate immediately after you are done.** I read this in a Dave Crenshaw's LinkedIn post and fell in love immediately. What do you do when you finish that important meeting? Jump right into the important report you have to finish, and from there you get into another meeting; you know the flow. But you don't need to jump from one thing to another like crazy. Once you've cleared your plate, avoid rushing to fill it again.

Maybe a good time to take a quick 5-min break?

Is it going to be perfect every single day? Absolutely... not. You'll have days where you might need to go a bit longer than usual, or catch up with delayed tasks. It's part of the game. Just be careful to not make this exception your rule.

PRO TIP

BOOK IT TO KEEP IT

Open your calendar and book one recurrent 15-min break mid-morning and another recurrent 15-min break mid-afternoon.

If it's not in your calendar is not happening.

Now you know the power of breaks and have a plan to manage your energy, but how do you protect it?

07

HOW ABOUT SAYING NO?

CHAPTER 7

―――――――――

"The level of your commitment is measured not by what you say yes to, but what you say no to"

- Rich Litvin

Everybody talks about boundaries.

How many times have you heard *'oh, you should set some boundaries'* or *'what's wrong with Ana? she needs to understand how to respect the boundaries of people'*. I've said things like that tons of times, I have even given it as advice.

And it's true, we all need to set boundaries. But of all the things I've had to do to become a productive person, this has been the hardest to adopt.

I have a confession to make: I failed for a long time to follow my own advice. I knew it was important, I knew it was slowing me down, but I just couldn't do it. Not because I didn't believe in it, but because I was looking at it from the wrong angle. I was setting boundaries thinking of others.

The biggest truth about boundaries: boundaries are meant for you, not for others! Let me say it again: **<u>boundaries are meant for you, not for others</u>.**

Once I started setting boundaries, everything fell into place like Tetris.

And what's the best boundary you have: saying no.

I know, it's hard. It makes you feel guilty. But if you say yes to every request and every favor, you will end up working on others priorities.

Imagine this: you plan to drive from Madrid to Paris to see the Eiffel tower for the first time. You are so excited! On the way you picked some people who are asking for a drive to Paris (you are a nice person after all). Suddenly someone asks to go first to Barcelona, then a quick stop in Marseille, and another in Lyon. If you say yes to all you will end up in Paris not in 14 hours, but in 3 days!

Same happens with your plans when you say yes to everything. People will assume you'll always say yes and always ask for your help, some even will play it in their favor. How do I know? Because I was a yes person.

You have to learn to say no to focus on what matters to you. At the beginning it doesn't feel good to say no when someone asks for something, but you don't have to feel guilty. Saying no is a skill, and as any skill, the more you do it the better you become at it.

WHERE TO START?

The hardest part it's always the first step, but to help you to make it easier, here's a few tips:

- **Just start**. The best way to be good at saying no? Start doing it.

- **Keep it short**. Don't over-explain, don't apologize. Short and sweet.

- **Don't make it personal**. Never make the reason about the other person. If you can't help on that project don't go with *'that's your project so it's your responsibility, not mine'*. Instead go for *'I would love to help but I'm already at 100% with my projects'*.

- **Offer and alternative.** This will give room to be helpful even when saying no. *'I would love to help but I'm already at 100% with my projects. <u>However, I'll be more than happy to have a coffee and brainstorm solutions when you feel stuck</u>'*

- **Do it early** – Don't delay the no if you already know what you want to say. Rip off the Band-Aid as quickly as possible.

By the way, saying no also applies to yourself. Say no to that extra episode of your favorite show so you can go to the gym. Say no to that funny video on TikTok to work on that personal project you've been postponing for months.

PRO TIP

SAY NO TO EVERYTHING NEXT WEEK

In the next few weeks practice saying no to every new request for extra things to do that comes your way (does not apply for key priorities at work).

Resist the urge to be the guy saving the day. The idea is to practice saying no so it will feel easier and more natural in the future.

And remember, short and sweet.

A final advice: make it sound natural. Avoid sounding like you are annoyed by the request or in a bad mood.

And talking about mood…

08

BE MOODY

CHAPTER 8

"The most important decision you make is to be in a good mood"

- Voltaire

How do you feel today? How about yesterday? and last week?

We don't feel the same every single day, and same happens with our mood. Some days you feel inspired, like nothing can stop you. Some others not that much.

And when you feel like doing nothing, how easy is it to do something? Not at all.

I've always wanted to be a writer, it's one of my biggest dreams. Every time I think about it I feel incredible, full of energy and joy; but for some time, when it came the moment to actually sit and write, I couldn't find the same inspiration I felt when thinking about it.

When I started I had days I was on fire, me and the pages alone for hours. After a couple of weeks, I had days when I felt off, tired, with zero inspiration. So, I ended up postponing it for when I felt inspired again.

What happened? 6 days out of 7 I just didn't do anything at all.

I was so frustrated, and it went like that for years.

It's true that to get where you want to be you need to push yourself. That's a fact. But let's be honest, pushing yourself all the time is hard. Nobody wants to live pushing themselves all day, every day. I was convinced there has to be a better way to help you push.

I'M NOT IN THE MOOD

After years of looking and trying different things I read *'match the task to your mood'*.

At the beginning I thought it was crazy but for some reason got stuck in my head for weeks, so I decided to give it a try... and now is the best trick I have to push myself.

Sounds great, right? You will only do the work you feel like doing!

Not exactly.

Sometimes you feel creative and inspired, other times you're maybe more in analytical mode. When you feel like you don't have the right 'mood' to do what's on your calendar think about your mood and pick a task from your ACTION LIST that matches it. Let say you have to prepare a presentation to convince your boss about a new project, but you don't feel creative when the reminder pops-up. What do you do? pick something form your list that doesn't required to be creative and do that.

I know what you are thinking: *'what if I'm in the mood of not doing anything at all?'*. Well, might be a good time for some low brain-power activity like those boring administrative tasks: checking your inbox, cleaning your ACTION LIST, filling that quarterly survey.

Or if everything is under control, why not just take a break from the craziness of the day?

PRO TIP

TAKE YOUR MOOD TO ANOTHER LEVEL

*Block a couple of fixed slots in your calendar and call it **mood time**. When the **mood time** comes, take an action from your ACTION LIST that matches your mood at that moment and work on that one.*

You have an urgency to take care of? No problem, just move it to another time.

*

Now you have your Time and Energy ingredients. You are almost there.

But there is another ingredient that without it you'll waste your productivity dish.

PART 3

Focus

09

NO FOCUS = WASTED TIME & ENERGY

CHAPTER 9

"The successful warrior is the average man, with laser-like focus"

- Bruce Lee

A lot of successful people talk about time, some about energy, and all of them about how they save time and energy to work on their dreams. It's like the new human currency.

And that's amazing. Every opportunity you have invest time and energy on the things you want to achieve for the life you want!

But…

… there's one additional ingredient that without it it's like baking a cake without eggs.

After years of learning and implementing what I've learnt about the first 2 ingredients of my productivity recipe, I was killing it! I was working my 9-5 job and during the evening building my own coaching service. My colleagues asked me how I was able to deal with my job and my personal projects and still feel energetic and ready to go every single day.

I felt incredible!

First week of January 2019, time for my yearly review after the Christmas break. All my projects at work running perfectly and working on my personal projects during the evenings. Everything was in order.

However, for some reason the needle was still not moving as much as I wanted, and I went from feeling incredible to frustrated. How it was possible if I was managing my time and energy so well. What was going on?

It took me some weeks but it hit me, and hard. I did have my time and energy under control, but I was wasting both working on lots of things at the same time.

I used to love multitasking. It made me feel I was moving twice as fast, preparing that critical presentation while in a meeting and then at home creating social media content while preparing other materials. I felt that I was being the most efficient person in the world.

The reality? I was moving in circles. I did manage my time and energy, but I was doing it without channeling neither of both.

That's why focus is so important. If you work on several things at the same time you are wasting your time AND energy. You might be working on quantity but you are sacrificing the quality of what you do.

HOW DO YOU FOCUS?

If you google about focus you'll find a ton of information about it, from the ultimate trick to the miraculous solution. But the trick is simple, and I'm sure you've heard it like a million times: **DON'T MULTITASK.**

That's it. The way to nail focus is to put your full attention to the task at hand, one task at a time.

When you are constantly switching between tasks constantly you are resetting the energy you need to start again.

Imagine you are on your driving home and your car stopped one block away from home. What would be easier:

1) Push a bit, stop & check your email, push again, stop to check if someone texts you and push again until you get home? or...

2) Push once and use the momentum to get home?

The irony of focus is that people think of focus as a thing, *'you should get more focus, try to put more focus on what you do'*.

In reality focus is an action. You don't get it, **YOU DO IT!**

The challenge is that our brain is desperate to save energy, and as focusing on one thing takes a ton of energy, it prefers to be relaxed. This is why it's easier and feels better to sit and watch one more episode of *The Blacklist* than to write the next chapter of your book (yeap, that's exactly what happened to me... and still happens some days).

So, from now on, let's **MONOTASK**.

But to do that, you need to fight the worst enemy of focus.

10

DISTRACTIONS

CHAPTER 10

"There are always distractions, if you allow them"

- Tony La Russa

Doesn't matter what's our job, focus is a must have to get s#!t done. We all know that. But, despite knowing, we are still so bad at it.

Might not be your fault. We live in a world that is constantly ON with our work plugged in our phones and with tons of things demanding our attention: our family, our jobs, social media, emails, messages, TV.

Yes, you can't control any of those, but you have a defense against them: **REMOVE DISTRACTIONS.**

I know it sounds cliche and that a lot of people say it, but you know why? Because it works!

Imagine this: You have to finish the end of year recap presentation for your boss and you only have 2 hours. How much will you get done if you work on those while checking your Instagram, your emails and that funny video your friend sent you? Most likely not that much.

Now, what if you put your phone away, take 50 min and put your full attention to work only on the presentation, take a break for 5 min, and then another 50 min of focused work? You'll be way closer to the finish line.

Sounds good, isn't it? But maybe you are thinking *'yes, sounds good, but easier said than done'*. And you know what, you are right.

But there are ways to make it easier for you. And to prove it to you here are 3 simple tips to work distraction free:

- **Take away the usual suspects**. Put away your phone, close your browser if you don't need it and turn-off email and message alerts on your PC. Be the boss of your devices.

- **Clean your desk.** The more things you have on your desk, the more distractions you have. The water bill, that info you printed to read later, your ACTION LIST. Do you need all of them while working on the end of year recap presentation? Not really. Find a place to keep them until you need them.

- **Find a space**. The majority of the workspace today is an open space, which makes interactions with colleagues easier… but also opens the door to interruptions when we want to do some focused work. Find a space in your office where you can 'hide' while finishing that report. How about at home? Have a dedicated space for work only. Working from your couch might be super comfy, but it's also a magnet for distractions.

The challenge here is that we all think: *'I don't need that, I can control it'*. And you probably can, but our brain is extremely bad at using our willpower. **It's easier to avoid temptations than to fight them**.

Talking about things we are bad at; how would you rate yourself at prioritizing?

11

PRIORITIES

CHAPTER 11

"People who can focus, get things done. People who can prioritize, get the right things done"

- John Maeda

Focused work without distractions is critical, but when you add priorities it channels your attention.

When I started my personal journey I worked on building a coaching service, posting on my website and creating content for social media. Then, after a few months, started a podcast and interviewed people on my Instagram. I was doing lots of things, on top of my 9-5 job, and I felt I was making so much progress!

But after 2 years I had to stop. I was feeling lost and stressed instead of excited for working on my personal projects. I took some time to think about it and after a couple of weeks realized I was working extremely focused on a lot of things without any particular priority.

I was not moving forward at all. I was not even working on my biggest dream!

So, I did what I should have done since the beginning: **prioritize**. And that's when I started to work on what was really important for me. Without setting my priorities I would never have started to write this book.

Setting priorities is one of the most critical habits you can have, but we mainly face 2 challenges when prioritizing.

The first challenge is that we suck at it. Prioritize is one of those things we think we are good at but in reality we are on the other side of the scale.

The second challenge is that is not the same every day. How many times have you set your priorities and it's easier today and then quite hard tomorrow? You will have days when it feels easier to prioritize and know exactly what's important, and other days when you'll feel a bit lost. That's life.

And if you add the fact that there are so many techniques to prioritize it can also be confusing: Eisenhower matrix, Ivy Lee method, MoSCoW technique, RICE score. They're all good and useful. In fact, feel free to try them. But for me, they make prioritization more complicated than it should be.

To prioritize all you need is to know what's important for you.

Remember the gathering phase? That's your best ally to prioritize. Here the gathering steps as a reminder:

1. List all the projects and goals you have: work, personal, family.

2. <u>Pick your 3 most important goals or projects</u>

3. <u>Take one of those goals and list all the actions that will help you to make it happen.</u>

4. Repeat step 3 for the other 2 goals

Why are steps 2 & 3 underlined this time? Because they are the key to prioritize: Step 2 gives you your most important projects and step 3 shows you the most immediate actions you can take.

ANYTHING VS. EVERYTHING

The biggest misconception today is the belief that to achieve you have to overdo. It might sound logical, *'the more I do the more I achieve, right?'* Well, not really. This mindset only leads to stress, feeling exhausted, and in some cases to burnout. **YOU CAN DO ANYTHING, BUT YOU CAN'T DO EVERYTHING.**

It's a misconception but it's not a lost cause, as there are some 'weapons' you can use to fight this overdo madness:

- **Prioritize first, plan after**. Some people like to do the planning and prioritization at the same time. If that has been working for you keep it. But if you are like me and other million people who struggles with setting priorities, it's easier and more efficient in the long run if you separate both. It makes the prioritization better and the planning easier.

- **Important over urgent**. Urgencies will always be part of the game, but don't confuse urgent with important. If you are not careful, urgent will push important away.

- **Enthusiasm ≠ important.** Just because it feels like a great opportunity at the moment doesn't mean it is. Write it on your MASTER LIST, let it cool off for a few days and then see what the real priority is with a calm mind.

- **Less is more.** I learnt this concept from the book *Essentialism* by Greg McKeown. Instead of *'how can I do everything I have to'* ask yourself *'which can I give my all to get the best result'* and work on that. We all have lots of things to do and want to do a lot of things… but do they all have the same weight and the same impact? Absolutely not! Work on the things that have the highest impact on your goals and don't overload yourself.

Having clear priorities and a structure to plan your things is important, but you also need to…

12

FIND YOUR FLOW

CHAPTER 12

"Concentration is the secret of strength"

- Ralph Waldo Emerson

High performers of every discipline are great at what they do. Not only because they train for it, work with no distractions and have clear priorities. They have something else, a secret to perform at the highest level: they are immersed in the moment, 100% in the task at hand. It's what sport players call 'the zone'.

If you want to be at your peak in everything you do you have to find a way to be in your zone. Once you are distractions free and clear on your priorities, you need to find that state of mind where you are 100% involved and committed with what you have to do.

Have you noticed that when you are doing something you enjoy you don't think about anything else and time seems to fly? That's how it feels to be in the zone.

Can we be in that state with everything we do? Absolutely!

Do we all know how to do it? Unfortunately, no. Nobody teaches us how to do it.

I struggled with this for a year. When I decided to start writing this book I booked time in my calendar, set my priorities and removed all distractions. I was ready and everything was in place, but for some reason I couldn't concentrate on writing. I had so many things in my mind I could not put one word after the other. I felt like a lot of people feel: *'writing it's not my thing, who am I kidding?'*

So, I stopped.

Five months passed after COVID restrictions and I found an article about finding your flow. The author (I forgot his name) explained how athletes like Kobe Bryant and Michael Phelps use it to be the best.

I felt inspired and decided to give it a try. It was a bit hard at the beginning, but after 2 weeks of practicing I found my flow… and now nothing can stop me!

WHERE TO START?

There's so much information about this that you can spend weeks reading about it. But to help you save some days of research here are the 3 tricks that has been the key for me and the people I've helped to find their flow:

- **Monotask**. You already saw it in chapter 9, but it is so critical that it's worth mentioning it again and again. I've seen this for years: people checking their email while in a meeting and then lost after the call, or working on 2 presentations and 1 report switching from one to another and then complaining they don't have time. Want to find your flow? Don't multitask.

- **Make it 50-5**. You can be in the zone only for a limited time. Do you imagine Michael Phelps swimming at top speed for 10 hours? Same with you. Different researches have shown that we can concentrate for only around 90 to 120 min, so the best we can do is to work in blocks. There are tons of techniques for this, being the most famous the pomodoro technique[5]. It helps, but in my experience 25 mins is too short. I have a technique

---

[5] The Pomodoro ® Technique utilizes fixed time intervals for focused work, usually 25 minutes, followed by short breaks.

I call 50-5 that has been my best ally to be in my zone: work for 50 min, pause for 5 min. What if your task takes more than 50 min? Work for 50, pause for 5, work again for 50, pause again for 5, and repeat as many times as needed.

- **Turn on the music.** Music is your best friend. Find a playlist that helps you concentrate, focus and get in the zone. I have 2 in Spotify: at work I listened to *Focus Flow*, and my go-to playlist to write is *Morning Study*. And as a great friend of mine says, feel free to steal with pride (thanks Dag!).

*

Your recipe it's almost done!

Get control of your days, channel your energy and find your flow. You know what you have to do…

…but do you know how to do it?

PART 4

Growth

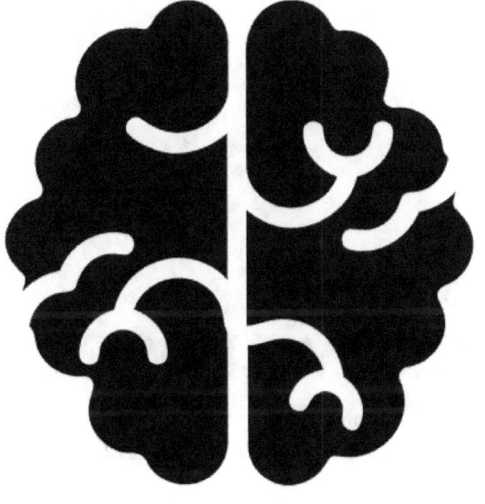

13

KNOWLEDGE IS FREEDOM

CHAPTER 13

"Growth today is an investment for tomorrow"

- John C. Maxwell

We talked about how to manage your time so you can be in control of your days, how to manage your energy so you can be at your best and how to remain focused to be in your zone.

However, there's still a missing ingredient to have the full productivity recipe and get to where you want to go.

I was particularly interested in climbing the corporate ladder. That was the definition of success when I graduated from the university back in 2008. *'If you don't have a good job and a good position you are a loser, a wasted talent'*. That's what people used to say.

I worked hard to get there. Attended every meeting, did everything that was assigned to me and volunteered to do other tasks my team struggled with. I was doing that religiously for years, but at some point, I realized I was not moving as much as I thought.

How's that possible if I was doing my job? I felt so frustrated! After a few days of feeling sorry for myself I took the easy explanation: I thought it was my manager's fault and complained about the unfairness of the situation.

After years of complaining and feeling like a victim I started to be honest with myself. I realized that the only way to move up was doing things beyond my work. So, I asked myself: *Jaime, what do you need to go beyond where you are?* and BAM! clear as water: I need to grow!

Michael Jordan is arguably one of the best basketball players in NBA history and one the best players in the history of sports. That's why you hear: '*that player? he is the Michael Jordan of [put any sport you like here]*'. But what makes Jordan this sport icon?

He was not the fastest, the strongest, the tallest nor the most talented. When he was a teenager, he was rejected from the school basketball team (could you imagine?). He was not even the first pick in the NBA draft.

WHAT'S THE SECRET FOR GREATNESS?

His secret? His mentality. He was working harder than anyone else, but more importantly, he was always improving his game and his skills. That's what made him the best.

That's the last B2P ingredient: **A GROWING MINDSET**.

But how do you get it?

Well, start doing more than what you have to do. To grow you have to face new challenges, learn new things and improve what you know. Growth is like a coin; it has 2 sides: **learning and improving**.

It works exactly the same as muscles, if you go to the gym and always lift the same weights you'll be great at the exercises you do; but if you want your muscles to grow you have to change the routine you do (learn) and lift heavier weights (improve)

You've probably heard a million times '*to grow you need to go outside of your comfort zone*'. I love this advice, because it's so true. Well, to some extent. I actually prefer to call it slightly different: **expand your comfort zone**.

Feeling uncomfortable all the time is not fun. True that you need to feel uncomfortable to grow, but you also deserve to enjoy what you learn. So, face that new challenge, embrace the discomfort of growing and then give you permission to enjoy the results.

Bad news: you could feel lost trying to find a way to expand your comfort zone.

Good news: there's a simple way to do it.

If you are happy where you are today, great! keep going!

But if you feel that there's more you could do and you have a dream you want to reach, but not sure on how to make it happen, here are some tips to help you in your journey to expand your comfort zone:

- **Start with why**. We all rush into what we need to do. You might even go one step further and plan on how you'll do it. But we (almost) never think about why we do it. If you don't know why you want to do it, you won't get there. Start with your purpose in mind and the what and how will follow.[6]

---

[6] For more about this get a copy of the book '*Start with Why*' from Simon Sinek.

- **There's no finish line**. This is one of the hardest realities nobody tells you about growing (and life): once you overcome a challenge there's a bigger challenge waiting for you. This is why you need to be in constant growth, to be ready for another round.

- **Becoming is better than being**. This is one of the best pieces of advice I can give you. The person that will get you where you want to be is the YOU of tomorrow, so look for opportunities to become that better version of yourself. Don't **be** the person who wants to write a book, **become** a writer!

Every phase of your life and career requires a different you, and the best way to start building that new you is by learning.

14

LEARNING

CHAPTER 14

"Anyone who keeps learning stays young"

- Henry Ford

How many championships and awards do you think Michael Jordan would have won if he thought that he learned everything when he won the first one in 1991? or how many gold medals you think Michael Phelps would have won if he thought there was nothing else to learn about swimming when he won the first medal in Athens in 2004.

They could have stopped right there. They were at the top of their game and of everyone else. They could have thought there was no one better than them and that they have learned every little detail about their sport. They have reached the top after all.

But…

They did the opposite. They didn't relax. They kept learning, perfecting their game until their last game. That is what made them the greatest at what they do.

Why don't we do the same?

We all want to be great at something. We dream of becoming someone and be recognized as an expert. But we also stop learning because we feel we know everything there is to know. And that's where we get stuck. We sabotage ourselves.

There is so much to learn. In today's world everything evolves so fast that would be insane to say that you know everything. How would you feel if your doctor stops learning about the new discoveries in medicine?

While we say *'I know everything there is to learn here, I'm an expert'* there is someone somewhere saying *'what else can I learn today'*.

IT'S EASIER THAN IT SOUNDS

With the infinite amount of information out there it can feel overwhelming… but it doesn't have to be.

Here a couple of tricks to help you on the learning front:

- **Be always a student.** There is a never-ending menu of learning possibilities: a new language, new discoveries in your field, new skills. Remember when you were studying and you finally understood what you thought was impossible to learn? You can still have that feeling. The more things you learn the more keys you'll have to open more doors.

- **Never assume you are an expert.** When you believe you are an expert is when you stop being one. There is a physiological effect called Dunning-Kruger effect[7], which says people wrongly overestimated their knowledge or ability in specific areas. Experts don't call themselves experts, they are always learning. Don't be a Dunning-Kruger.

---

[7] David Dunning, Justin Kruger. *Unskilled and unaware of it: how difficulties in recognizing one's own incompetence lead to inflated self-assessments.* Journal of personality and social psychology. November 30, 1999.

- **The best teacher: Failure**. We are living in a time when failure is an identity. When we fail, we think *'I'm a failure'*. Failing feels like s#!t, not going to lie to you, but you can't let failure define you. Every time you fail the teacher is trying to tell you something: this is how not to do it; this is what you need to learn. Setbacks are just a wakeup call.

PRO TIP

GIVE YOURSELF PERMISSION TO FEEL LIKE S#!T

Next time you fail, take your time and feel what you have to feel. The next day? No more whining, just keep moving.

Learning new things helps you to be better, and to grow you also need to be in constant evolution.

But how do you evolve?

15

YOU VS. YOU

CHAPTER 15

"It never ceases to amaze me: we all love ourselves more than other people, but care more about their opinion than our own."

- Marcus Aurelius

What made Muhammad Ali the greatest boxer, Jordan the greatest basketball player, Phelps the best swimmer, Federer the best tennis player? They were constantly improving.

That's what makes greats great, always improving what they do, what they know. And that is exactly what we all failed to do.

For years I was always looking at what others were doing. Looking at what others had that I hadn't, what they knew that I didn't. The result? Frustration. I felt I was not good enough and life was not good to me. I was not taking advantage of who I was, what made me unique.

I was doing the right thing for the wrong reason. I was pursuing an impossible destination.

If you were able to do whatever you want, would you still compare yourself to that colleague that **<u>seems</u>** to be doing better than you?

YOU ARE COMPETING AGAINST THE WRONG PLAYER

We've all done it, and it feels that everything around us is pushing us to do it. But comparing with others it's a recipe for disaster and a guarantee to not get where you want to be.

The game of life is a 1on1 game, and it's a game of **YOU VS. YOU**. Do you think Federer focused on Rafael Nadal to improve his game? Or Jordan focused on Clyde Drexler to become the greatest of all time? (you don't know who Drexler is? there you go!) No. They worked on improving **<u>their</u>** skills, **<u>their</u>** technique, **<u>their</u>** game. If you want to become who **YOU** want to be you have to focus on **YOU**.

I know what you are thinking, because I thought the same: *'how do I eat this?'* Well, here a few tips I've learned to help you win your game:

- **Progress over goals**. This is the most important of all! Having goals is important but we can't be obsessed about it. Thinking about your goal will not help you move… but one step does. And the more you progress the more motivated you'll feel. It's a win-win!

- **Take action**. The only way to grow is by doing. Thinking about what you need to do or planning how you'll improve will not take you anywhere, even if it feels like it. *"Knowing what you need to do to improve your life takes wisdom, pushing yourself to do it takes courage"*[8]. How can you go to new and exciting places if you never leave your house?

- **Focus on strengths**. We all have strengths and weaknesses, but today's world seems to be obsessed with the latter. What is the typical performance review advice at any job? You need to work on your areas of opportunities (aka weaknesses). If something is slowing you down, work on it until it's not a problem anymore, but then keep working on

---

[8] Mel Robbins, *5 second rule.*

your strengths. That's how you grow. If you want to go from bad to good work on your weaknesses, but to move from good to great? Your strengths are the ones that will take you there.

- **Small is better than big.** You don't need to make huge leaps to improve. Small consistent steps will take you further than sporadic jumps (and make it easier to maintain progress). There's a concept called 1% better[9]: just improving 1% each day has a huge effect overtime. There's even a formula for this:

No improvement → $(1.00)365 = 1.00$

vs.

1% better a day for a year → $(1.01)365 = 37.78$

Which one do you prefer?

- **There's no roof.** We stop improving because we feel we reach 'our capacity'. In reality we are not even close! You will always find a way to improve your strengths. There's no finish line when it comes to improving!

---

[9] James Clear, *Atomic Habits*

PRO TIP

REFLECT ON HOW IT'S GOING

When was the last time you took time to think about how things are going, what have you done well and what could you do better?

Give yourself the time to escape from the details of everyday tasks and see the big picture regularly. 30 min each week is a great place to start.

Now you are learning new things and improving what you know. But there's a ghost that follows all of us saying: *'what if you don't have the talent?'*. Well, talent could give you an advantage, but talent alone will not get you where you want to be.

So, if it's not talent, what is it?

16

TALENT OR EFFORT?

CHAPTER 16

"Hard work beats talent when talent doesn't work hard"

- Tim Notke

We all know talented people. They make things look easy when they do it but feel extremely hard when we try it.

If you see Messi plays (or Cristiano Ronaldo if you prefer) it's like everybody else is an amateur. They might have some innate talent since they were kids but both work very hard, even more than the rest, to be where they are.

In my experience, effort beats talent all the time. Talent could give you an edge, especially at the beginning, but if you rely only on talent and don't work hard to improve, you're setting a limit to yourself. Talent is what it is, but practice has a growth effect that talent does not have.

Kobe Bryant is a great example. He started playing basketball in Italy when he was a kid, but he was not a good player. Other kids showed more talent, but he was determined. He invested more hours than any other kid to improve his game. He practiced during summer vacation while other kids were having fun. What happened? He not only became a better player than the rest of the boys in Italy, but ended up having a spot among the greatest who ever played.

Now, you might be thinking: *'but Jaime, I don't feel I have what it takes'*. And you know what, we all feel like that. More than what we would like to accept. But if you never try, you'll never know.

This book is the best example I can give you. I almost didn't write it. I dreamt about writing a book since I was a kid. Then as an adult I thought about that dream from time to time but never started. I felt that you need a special talent to be a writer, like Hemingway or García Márquez, and I always ended up putting it in the parking lot.

One day I decided to give it a try and start. I put in the effort to write consistently, especially the days I didn't feel like it. I'm not going to lie and tell you it was easy. It took me a lot of push, a lot of effort, a lot of fights with myself when I didn't feel like showing up, but it was all worth it… and here you have it in your hands.

Fun fact: I still believe I'm not a naturally talented writer, but practice and effort has helped me to become writer.

HOW TO MAKE AN EFFORT?

If you look for the definition of effort, you'll find *'physical or mental activity needed to achieve something, or energy used to do something'*[10]. And maybe that's why we tend to avoid the effort, because we tend to prefer to save energy.

The key to make it happen is to make effort sustainable, and the secret to do it is discipline. Why? Because you fall in love with your goal but that does not mean you'll like what you have to do every single day.

---

[10] Cambridge Dictionary.
https://dictionary.cambridge.org/dictionary/english/effort

I love writing, but there are days where I just don't want to do it and rather watch another episode of Lucifer with my wife and my dogs in the comfort of my couch with a warm cup of coffee. But I pushed myself to stand up and write because otherwise you wouldn't be reading this book and I'd still be dreaming about becoming a writer.

There's a quote from Mike Tyson that changed the way I see discipline: *'Discipline is doing what you hate to do but do it like you love it'*

Perseverance overcome talent when talent is not developed[11]. If you have a talent and don't put the effort to improve it, people with less talent but with the perseverance to keep pushing will surpass you.

---

[11] Angela Duckworth, *GRIT*

So, show up, put one foot in front of the other and practice, practice and practice. **Put in the effort every day and see yourself becoming who you thought you couldn't be**.

PART 5

Now what?

THE B2P SYSTEM

CHAPTER 17

"Some people want it to happen, some wish it would happen, others make it happen"

- Michael Jordan

THANK YOU for going this far.

And **CONGRATULATIONS!**

You are ready to cook your own **B2P** recipe and move from **BUSY TO PRODUCTIVE**.

If you jumped directly here you can start using the system and enjoying the benefits, but I encourage you to read the book as it has the key principles that will help you to maintain your system up and running over time.

BELIEVE IN SIMPLE

We are so used to a complex world with lots of processes and tools that when we see something simple, we don't believe it's possible. **I WANT YOU TO CHALLENGE THAT**.

That's why I developed the B2P system, to help you believe that simple can help you move closer to your goals.

But is not just a system, it's a simple system.

How simple?

THIS SIMPLE:

1. **LIST it**. List everything you want to achieve or complete: all your goals, projects, objectives. This is your **MASTER LIST.**

2. **PRIORITIZE it**. From your MASTER LIST take the 3 most important projects you want or need to complete.

3. **EXPAND it.** For each of your 3 priorities list all the actions you can think of that will help you to complete them. Think of simple, manageable actions and be as specific as possible (remember, if too big break it into pieces). This is your **ACTION LIST.**

4. **PICK it.** From all the actions you listed, pick the most immediate ones you can take care of.

5. **BOOK it.** Book your immediate actions in your calendar. Go as far as you want.

6. **REPEAT it**. Once you complete all your immediate actions, repeat.

That's it! Short and sweet.

You might be thinking that to make it work you need a lot of stuff and information. And the reality is… absolutely not!

Remember the only 2 things you need to be productive? That's all you need for your B2P system: a notebook and a calendar.

That's the beauty of the B2P system, that you don't need additional information, complicated steps or updating software and tools. The system will help you in a very simple way to plan what you need to do and to take action, that's it.

<u>Now you have your B2P system to help you move forward.</u>

LET'S DO AN EXPERIMENT TOGETHER

I want to do a quick 2-min exercise with you.

Think of all the things you have to do and want to do, everything you have on your mind: finishing that big presentation for your project, the end of the year report for your boss, do the laundry, read more, exercise, eat healthier, clean the attic. <u>Don't write anything down.</u>

How do you feel?

Now **grab your notebook and a pen** and write down all of the things you thought about, all of them.

How do you feel now?

You've probably felt overwhelmed after thinking about all the things you have to do. That's how we live every day, with all the things we have to do running at full speed in our mind, piling up on our subconscious.

But after writing them down you feel way less overwhelmed, even refreshed. That's what a B2P life feels like, having a free mind that doesn't have to worry about remembering everything you have on your plate.

We all deserve to have a life like that, and that's why the B2P system is perfect for everybody: people starting their careers, organization leaders and business owners. No matter what you do, you can benefit from this and adapt it to your lifestyle.

And as the only way to take a plan out of the paper is by taking action, how about putting what you learnt into practice?

Bonus chapter

1-WEEK B2P BOOTCAMP

CHAPTER 18

"You don't rise to the level of your goals, you fall to the level of your systems"

- James Clear

Welcome to the B2P training camp!

You made it. And you have all you need to become a productive person.

But I know changing is not easy. It can feel so overwhelming not knowing where to start, how to start, how to make it work.

I know because I've felt all of that. It took me 11 years to implement everything I shared with you in this book and to make a plan that helped me to put all of it together.

And I want to share with you that plan to help you do that… **IN JUST 7 DAYS!**

Are you ready to take control of your days and start moving from busy to productive? Are you excited? I AM! Let's do it.

THE PLAN

For the next 7 days you are going to take some actions of the B2P bootcamp <u>per day</u> to challenge the way you've been managing your time and energy.

You might feel tempted to do more in one day, as some of the actions are easy to complete, but to get the best out of it no cheating, only 1 day at a time!

And to make it easier, each day has a checklist

Let's get to day 1!

DAY 1 – CLEAN YOUR CALENDAR

Almost everything in life starts with a clean slate, and becoming productive is no different.

So, let's start easy: delete all the things you have in your calendar that you don't need. Don't know what it is? Gone; that useless meeting that you don't know why you have it, gone too.

- ☐ Remove what you don't need
- ☐ Remove unnecessary meetings
- ☐ Remove what you don't know

PRO TIP

GET RID OF THAT MEETING

If you are not sure about deleting a meeting (we all have those) here's a trick that works wonders: ask the owner of the meeting 'is there anything you need from me for this call?'

Yes, attend. No, decline. Only information, share it in advance and skip it.

DAY 2 - STRAT WITH YOUR ME-TIME

YOU ARE YOUR PRIORITY 1!

All those things that are for you that you know are important but never pay that much attention are the first you will book in your calendar.

- ☐ Book your lunch break
- ☐ Book your morning 15-min break
- ☐ Book your afternoon 15-min break

Bonus step:
- ☐ Book the time you want to stop working

DAY 3 - MAKE YOUR MASTER LIST

Time to GO-ACT.

And it starts with the Gather phase:

- ☐ Get your notebook
- ☐ Name 1 page **MASTER LIST**
- ☐ List all your projects
- ☐ List things you need to do
- ☐ List all the pending objectives you have hanging around

<u>Today is not about actions, only projects</u>

```
MASTER LIST

- My book
- Project Enzo
- Clean attic
- Project Circe
- Workshop B2P.
- Re-paint house
- End of year review
- Fix garden
- Project
```

DAY 4 - START YOUR ACTION LIST

Today you start to gather your actions:

- ☐ Pick the 3 most important projects from your **MASTER LIST**.

```
                    MASTER LIST

      - My book
      - Project ▬▬
      - Clean attic
      - Project ▬▬
      - Workshop B2P
      - Re-paint house
      - End of year review
      - Fix garden
      - Project ▬▬▬
```

- ☐ Name another page **ACTION LIST**

☐ Take 1 project and list all the actions you can think of that can help you to complete your project in your **ACTION LIST**. <u>Don't think about the order</u>

ACTION LIST

My book.

- Start writing routine
- Mind map overall ideas
- Outline book based on mind map
- Draft book
- Edit phase 1
- Edit phase 2
- Edit phase n?
- Design book cover
- Name the book
- Publish the book
- Promote the book
- Send copy to review group

from Busy to Productive | 133

DAY 5 - CLOSE YOUR ACTION LIST

And today you close the gathering phase:

- [ ] Take the other 2 projects from your **MASTER LIST**
- [ ] Pick one and list all the actions in your **ACTION LIST**.
- [ ] Repeat for the other project.

ACTION LIST

My book
- Start writing routine
- Mind map overall ideas
- Outline book based on mind map
- Draft book
- Edit phase 1
- Edit phase 2
- Edit phase n?
- Design book cover
- Name the book
- Publish the book
- Promote the book
- Send copy to review group

Project ~~~~
- Review historical data
- Draft learning plan
- Prepare action plan
- Brief agency
- Send LP for review
- Sign off LP
- Review results
- Prepare report
- Debrief team
- Archive report

End of year review
- Collect learnings
- Request feedback
- Draft review
- List top strengths
- List top opportunities
- Book review chat
- Update system
- Sign off review

<u>Remember, don't think about the order of the actions</u>

DAY 6 - PRIORITIZE

Today you close the GO-ACT

Now that you have all the steps for your most important projects in your ACTION LIST, let's get into the Organize phase:

- ☐ Review your ACTION LIST
- ☐ Pick the most immediate actions for the week ahead. <u>Don't think only big, just the ones that you can complete in the coming days, big or small</u>
- ☐ Book them in your calendar. <u>Remember to break big actions into smaller ones</u>
- ☐ Book your highlight of the day for each day
- ☐ Book your 3 30-min Urgency slots
- ☐ Book your 2 Mood Time slots

And for the Action phase, remember to:

→ Use the 5-sec rule to take action when the calendar reminder appears on your screen (page 34)
→ Follow the 2-min rule for quick actions (page 36)

PRO TIP

START WITH 1 HOUR

Sometimes it's hard to know how long to book for your actions. I recommend booking at least 1 hour per action to start and apply the 50-5 technique.

Not enough? Extend when needed. The more you do it the more accurate you'll become.

DAY 7 - ENJOY

You made it!

Time to forget about your lists, projects and calendar and enjoy the win. You deserve it!

Just remember to:

- → **Monotask, never multitask**
- → **Remove distractions**
- → **Don't overdue yourself**

*

By now you've worked on your recipe to become a productive person, have all the principles to make it sustainable over time and went through the B2P bootcamp in just 1 week.

You are officially ready to take control of your days!

Put it into practice every day, make it part of your routine and **HAVE A B2P LIFE!**

A huge THANK YOU!!

Thank you for honoring me with your valuable time. Thank you for learning with me. Thank you for being part of this journey.

If you have any questions or just want to have a chat, please feel free to reach out with an email: jaimesauret@gmail.com. I'll be more than happy to help you!

Have you heard that sharing is caring? Let's practice that: **<u>If you enjoyed this book, share it with someone else</u>**. Gift this book to that friend who is struggling to be in the driver seat of her life, or loan it to that colleague at work who needs help to be in control of his days.

You could make a huge difference in the life of someone else.

I wish you all the best on your journey moving
<u>FROM BUSY TO PRODUCTIVE</u>

FURTHER READING

If you want to read more about productivity, here are great books I've read and recommend to deep dive more into:

Time & Energy Management

Make Time, by Jake Knapp and John Zeratsky.

Rework, by Jason Fried and David Heinemeier Hansson.

Getting Things Done, by David Allen.

Mind Management, by David Kadavy.

Essentialism, by Greg McKeown.

The 5 Second Rule, by Mel Robbins.

Productivity & Growth mindset

The Compound Effect, by Darren Hardy.

Effortless, by Greg McKeown.

Atomic Habits, by James Clear.

Start with Why, by Simon Sinek.

Grit: The power of Passion and Perseverance, by Angela Duckworth.

Mindset: The New Psychology of success, by Carol S. Dweck

Level up your self-discipline, by Som Bathla

ACKNOWLEDGEMENTS

This book is about how to become a productive person and be control of your days. Ironically, I almost didn't write it. I doubt myself, felt victim of impostor syndrome and failed to follow some of my own advices and principles while writing it (we are all humans).

But thanks to the people that has been part of this journey you have it in your hands today.

That's why I can't finish this book without thanking all of you.

Leidi, thanks for being there for me every single day, pushing me when needed, refreshing my memory about why I started this and more importantly reminding me to have fun while doing it.

Mom, thank you for being there encouraging me to raise the bar and letting me know every day that I can always do more.

Juan, Dag, a huge THANK YOU for being my test readers, investing the time to read it and sharing your thoughts and feedback.

Ricardo, I know you couldn't read it, but thanks to you this book has the amazing cover it has, your ideas on the cover design were the inspiration to make it possible.

And to my friends, colleagues, clients, who have asked me about how the book was going a huge THANK YOU, you were the ones that make me come back when I didn't feel like writing.

WITHOUT ANY OF YOU THIS BOOK WOULD HAVE NEVER BEEN A REALITY!

B2P CORPORATE WORKSHOPS

Want to bring the B2P life to your organization? YOU CAN with the B2P corporate workshops for your team.

Do you work by yourself or want to have a more 1:1 session? I have options for you too!

Check www.jaimesauret.com for more information.

I would love to meet you!

JOIN THE B2P COMMUNITY

Follow me on my socials for tips and hacks to keep improving your productivity:

- → LinkedIn: jaimesauret
- → Threads: jaimesauret
- → X: jaimesauret

Or subscribe to the B2P VIP list to get exclusive weekly content on how to keep moving from busy to productive… and for free! Join at www.jaimesauret.com

ONE LAST THING

I'd love to hear what you think!

I really appreciate your feedback and love hearing what you have to say.

If you can take 2 minutes of your time to leave a helpful review on Amazon letting me know what you think about the book it will be super helpful. And if you are using Goodreads it will be great to have your review there as well!

I need your help to make the next version of this book and my future books better!

Thank you very much!!

Jaime Sauret

www.ingramcontent.com/pod-product-compliance
Lightning Source LLC
Chambersburg PA
CBHW071054240526
45471CB00015B/1855